SCHIRMER'S LIBRARY
OF MUSICAL CLASSICS

Vol. 1764

EIGHTEEN
ORIGINAL PIANO DUETS

By

Bizet, Dvořák, Fauré, Glière, Mussorgsky,

Rachmaninoff, Saint-Saëns, Stravinsky

Compiled
by
ERNO BALOGH

G. SCHIRMER, Inc.

DISTRIBUTED BY
HAL•LEONARD®
CORPORATION
7777 W. BLUEMOUND RD. P.O. BOX 13819 MILWAUKEE, WI 53213

CONTENTS

Five Easy Pieces

(Primo Easy)

1. Andante

Igor Stravinsky, 1917

Secondo

Five Easy Pieces

(Primo Easy)

1. Andante

Igor Stravinsky, 1917

Primo

2. Española

Secondo

2. Española

Primo

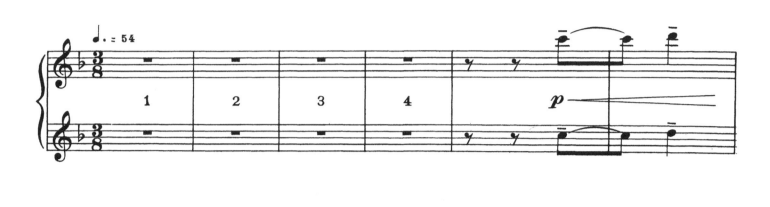

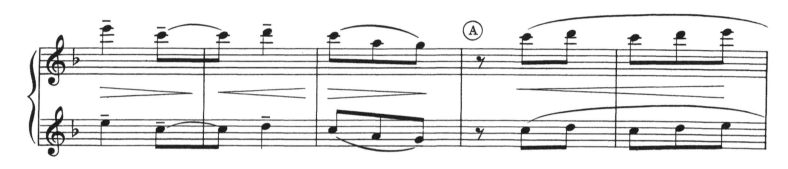

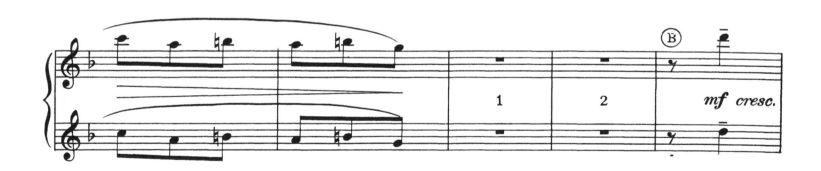

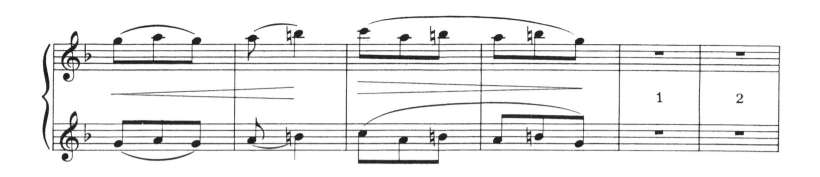

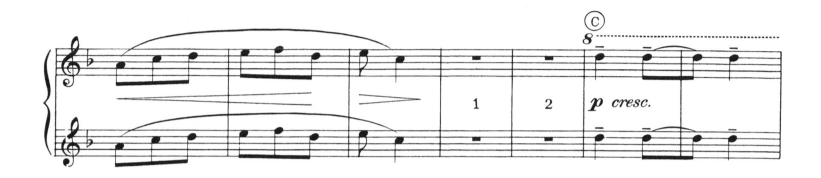

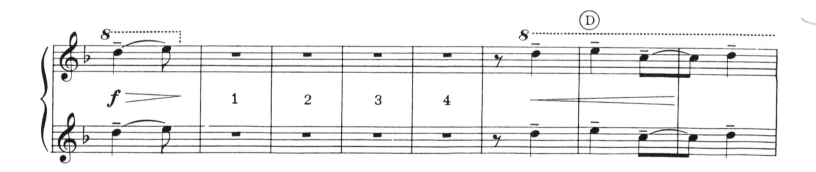

3. Balalaïka

Secondo

3. Balalaïka

Primo

4. Napolitana

Secondo

4. Napolitana

Primo

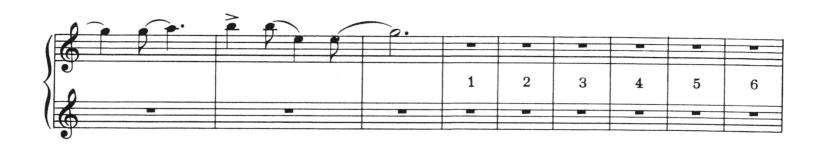

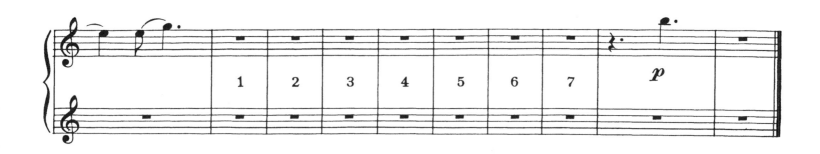

5. Galop

Secondo

5. Galop

Primo

Galoppo D.C.

Berceuse
from "Dolly"

Gabriel Fauré, Op. 56, No. 1

Secondo

Allegretto moderato

Berceuse

from "Dolly"

Gabriel Fauré, Op. 56, No. 1

Primo

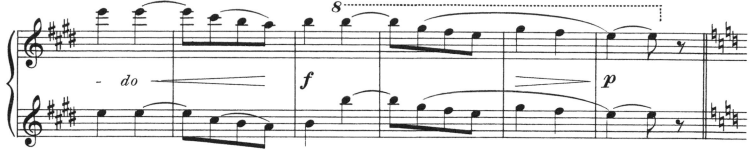

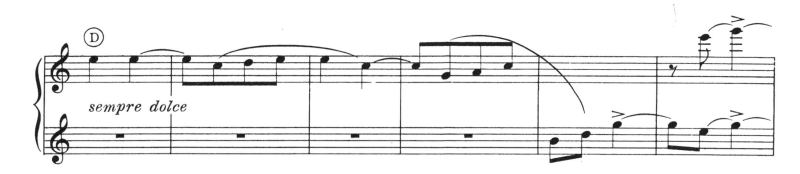

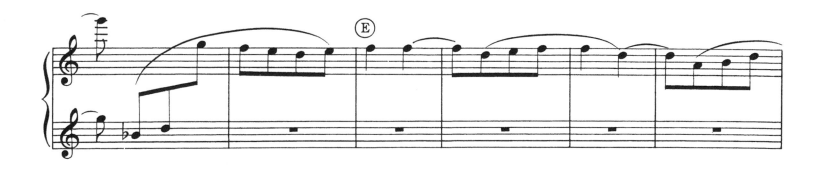

Little Husband, Little Wife!

from "Jeux d'Enfants"

Georges Bizet, Op. 22, No. 11

Secondo

Little Husband, Little Wife!
from "Jeux d'Enfants"

Georges Bizet, Op. 22, No. 11

Primo

Russian Song

Sergei Rachmaninoff, Op. 11, No. 3

Secondo

Andantino cantabile

Russian Song

Sergei Rachmaninoff, Op. 11, No. 3

Primo

The Doll
Berceuse from "Jeux d'Enfants"

Georges Bizet, Op. 22, No. 3

Secondo

The Doll

Berceuse from "Jeux d'Enfants"

Georges Bizet, Op. 22, No. 3

Primo

Three Easy Pieces

(Secondo Easy)

1. March

Igor Stravinsky, 1915

Secondo

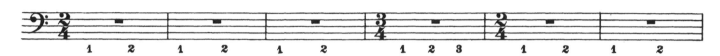

staccato throughout

Three Easy Pieces

(Secondo Easy)

1. March

Primo

Igor Stravinsky, 1915

2. Valse

Secondo

Fine

2. Valse

Primo

Fine

D.C. al fine

Trio

poco rubato

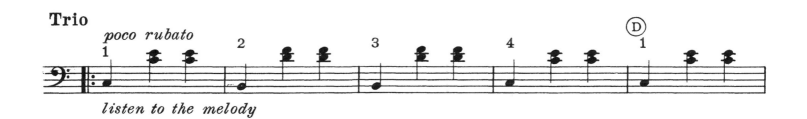

listen to the melody

D. C. al fine

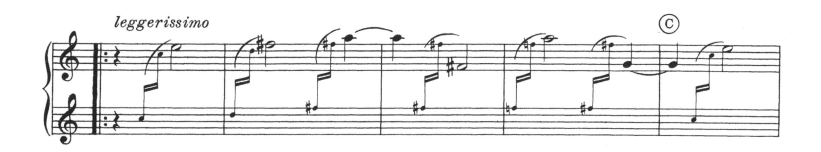

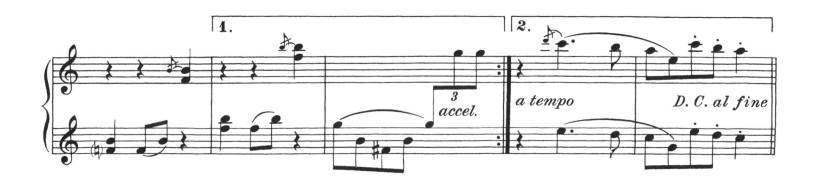

3. Polka

Secondo

3. Polka

Primo

Etude

Reinhold Glière, Op. 48, No. 5

Secondo

Etude

Reinhold Glière, Op. 48, No. 5

Primo

Scherzo

Reinhold Glière, Op. 48, No. 11

Secondo

Scherzo

Reinhold Glière, Op. 48, No. 11

Primo

Secondo

Slavonic Dance No. 10

Antonin Dvořák, Op. 72, Bk. I

Secondo

Slavonic Dance No. 10

Antonín Dvořák, Op. 72, Bk. I

Primo

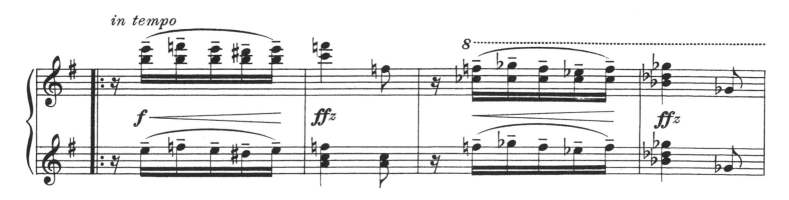

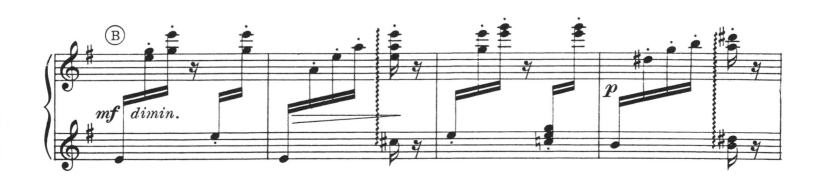

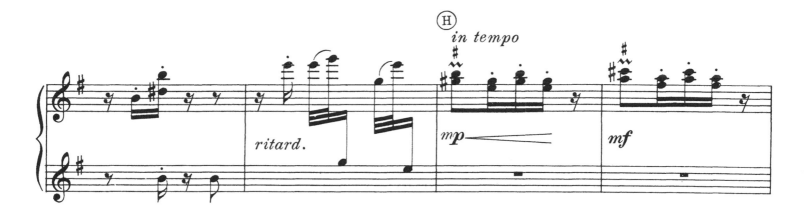

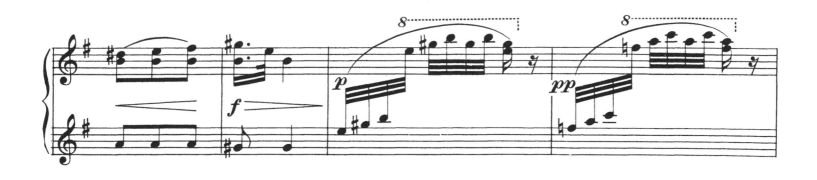

Slavonic Dance No. 2

Antonin Dvořák, Op. 46, Bk. I

Secondo

Allegretto scherzando

Slavonic Dance No. 2

Antonin Dvořák, Op. 46, Bk. I

Primo

Allegretto scherzando

Secondo

Più mosso

Secondo

Secondo

Pas Redoublé

Camille Saint-Saëns, Op. 86

Secondo

Pas Redoublé

Camille Saint-Saëns, Op. 86

Primo

Secondo

Secondo

Sonata

Modest Mussorgsky, 1860

I

Secondo

Sonata

Modest Mussorgsky, 1860

I

Primo

Secondo

II
Scherzo

Secondo

Allegro non troppo

II
Scherzo

Primo

Allegro non troppo

Poco meno mosso

Allegro non troppo (Tempo I)

Allegro non troppo (Tempo I)